REG KRAY'S BOOK OF

Slang

REG KRAY'S

BOOK OF

SIDGWICK & JACKSON
LONDON

First published in Great Britain in 1989
by Sidgwick & Jackson Limited
Originally published by
Wheel and Deal Publications

ISBN 0-283-99915-2

Photoset in Linotron Caledonia
by Rowland Phototypesetting Limited
Bury St Edmunds, Suffolk

Printed in Great Britain by
Butler and Tanner Ltd, Frome, Somerset

slang

CONTENTS

FOREWORD

by Patsy Manning

*Who spent one year with Reggie Kray
in Long Lartin Prison.*

Reggie Kray is in Lewes Prison, one of England's top security jails. He is serving a life sentence for one gangland murder with a recommendation to complete thirty years. He has been in prison now for twenty gruelling years. In my opinion that is cruelty, not punishment, because I know if they blew a hole in the wall Reg would not bother to escape; he's done far too long and would not ruin whatever slight chance he had of being paroled in the near future. Reg has always been interested in words – that's why a dictionary is always in easy reach so he can look up any word that is new to him. Reg passes most of his time writing and rarely looks at the television, but on one rare occasion when Reg did watch television he noticed a lot of slang had crept into the British and American scripts. This gave him the idea to write this book, *Slang*, so both ordinary British and American people could understand the slang phrases used by the underworld characters in television programmes such as *Minder*, *The Professionals* and American gangster films etc. This book will also be invaluable to directors and scriptwriters, on both sides of the Atlantic, who are engaged in making such films.

Reg hopes this book will help to enlighten all who read it.

slang

PATSY MANNING

Dedication by Reggie Kray

I first met Patsy Manning about thirty years ago outside my billiard hall in the Mile End Road.

We have been friends ever since. He is a lovable character and is a present-day Errol Flynn, full of adventure and a yearning for the ladies, and he has had plenty of both.

He was a bit of a rogue and turned to crooked ways out of adventure. But I urged him to go straight and he bet me he would travel the world, which he did, and he wrote a book on his journey and life called *Crumpet All the Way*.

I am sure the reader will become firm friends with Patsy just as I did. How can one not feel friendly towards a lovable rogue?

Patsy Manning.

REGGIE KRAY

Born 24 October 1933, convicted of murder
1969, sentenced to life imprisonment.
Age 56.
Hobbies: Writing.
Ambitions: to be recognised as an author,
and to live in the country.

INTRODUCTION

I had hidden myself under the blankets, soaking in sweat and
blood. I continued to saw away at my wrist with a broken piece
of glass, which I had broken from my TV spectacles. Eventually
I fell into a fitful sleep, only to awake the following morning
to the clang of the bolt being drawn across my cell door.

It seems that my prayers had been answered in a strange
sort of way, because prior to this attempted suicide, I had
calmly smoked what I thought to be my last cigarette, and said
a prayer. My state of mind stemmed from a period of time I
had spent at Long Lartin Prison, and my meeting up with a
foreigner, who in my opinion was an agent provocateur for his
own gain and ends, i.e. his quest to curry favour with the
authorities to secure himself early parole. He had attempted
to seduce me and introduce me to the smoking of hashish,
with the purpose of gaining information from me. When this
failed, I am sure that he introduced this drug into a curry that
he prepared for me. The result was that I suffered from an
intense feeling of paranoia, and that my conclusions were that
my family and I were friendless.

My state of paranoia made me feel, for no clear reason, that
I was responsible for this situation. At that time, for my family's

slang

sake, I decided to commit suicide. Peculiar as it may seem, I bear no malice towards this foreigner, he has taught me another lesson in the school of life. I do feel that he is a person of weak character. If he is reading this I would like him to know that I pray to Allah that he may give him strength.

I would like to make one thing quite clear, and that is, drugs at Long Lartin were almost non-existent, but like any large establishment, be it an airport or a customs zone, there is always a loophole to exploit, however small, for illegal contraband. This particular lacing of my food was a rare occurrence that I had come across.

After my transfer to the prison hospital, here at Parkhurst, I did a lot of self-analysis on my recovery from this bout of illness, even to the extent of making up a riddle about myself. My riddle goes:

I thought I was him
I thought I was he
But I am neither
I am the one in between.

This theory of mine came about, looking back on my two paths of good intent, and what have been called my evil deeds, which led me to believe, like the riddle said, I am neither but a part of each.

During my stay at the hospital at Parkhurst, I also gave a lot of thought to the young persons who are present throughout the complex world of prison society, and have come to the conclusion that the authorities could be more humane, if they were to realise that these youngsters need to be given short sharp sentences, similar to those of the detention centres for young offenders, because one can learn if one has any sense, within a year of any sentence, that prison life is a total waste of time, both physically and spiritually. One does not have to suffer six years or four years to have this lesson impressed on one's mind. Also I feel that more practical help in the way of financial assistance would benefit these young people.

Inasmuch that if they had an initial lift on release from prison, the state would be saved huge sums of money by stopping them becoming recidivists in their quest for gain, born out of desperation.

My other views on prison life surround the parole system. The radio and newspapers, and my own experience, tell me there is a crisis about to break in the prison system. To solve this problem of overcrowding, half remission should be brought in for all lengths of sentences, and once again the prison population would become stable; if not, as sure as night follows day, there will be a lot of trouble in prisons throughout the country. Inmates should also be personally interviewed by the parole board, instead of by the faceless officials of the Home Office.

I know the effects of long-term imprisonment, when one is cut off from friends and relations. In fact the pen became the instrument of my emotions, until recently when I was moved to the main wing at Parkhurst from the hospital wing, and have once again come into contact with many people. So at the moment I am quite happy in my surroundings. I have also come to terms with the essence of the time element, and so I enjoy each day and no longer wish the time away.

I am studying astronomy because fifteen years ago, I vowed to do so at the suggestion of my Queen's Counsel, Mr Paul Wrighton, at my trial. I also have many penfriends across the country, which helps me to keep occupied.

I have also written a keep fit book that should be published shortly.

Due to the fact that I have met good friends in this prison,

slang

I would not change anything of my past, except to be in the company of my late parents. As for my remorse that is a private and personal emotion.

Sometimes in the quiet of the night, when everyone is locked up, I theorise about the occupants of the different cells to my left and right, locked up with their dreams and frustrations in this human zoo.

Part of my philosophy has taught me never to think of those who gave evidence against me in their roles as Judas, because then I would be bitter and a loser. Because I never think of them I am a winner.

I also bear no malice or grudge against any of the police who arrested me, or the judge who sentenced me, because it was part of their job and profession, though I do feel that our sentences were too severe.

I do blame the use of drugs for the increasing crime rate, especially in the juvenile age group, who are not aware of the consequences. I have also found in prison many of these young offenders talk from the top of their heads, and lack tact and diplomacy, which can lead them into trouble, especially amongst themselves. They would have been in serious trouble had they lived in an area like the East End of London in the 1960s.

Unlike many of these youngsters, I am very tolerant towards my fellow inmates, because I have been through paranoia, where one thinks one is friendless, so now I look upon the bright side of people's personalities and make-up.

There is also much humour in prison life, as the tale of the lifer who bore a grudge against his brother, who had a beautiful garden in the suburbs. This particular lifer confessed to several murders, and said the bodies were buried in his brother's garden. Under this pretext the beautiful garden was dug up and he had evened the score with his brother, much to the dismay of the police, who only discovered flowerbeds and roots.

I go up for my Category A review in October, which is also the month of my birthday. This interview could hinder my chances of coming off the status of Category A, but to my way of thinking it should not do so, because no truth is ever a lie. I also go up for a lifer's review in July. I hope that one day the parole board will consider this proverb:

> One will never learn to swim,
> unless one goes into the water.
> As I will not be able to adapt
> again to Society unless given a
> chance to do so.

All long-term prisoners go through periods of time suffering from loss of identity. This is understandable when one thinks of people such as Sir Francis Chichester, who after a year at sea on his yacht, could not converse properly on arrival home, because of a personality disorder, brought about by being in solitude as a lone yachtsman. Also, there is the particular case of Brook, the Englishman, who was arrested in Russia for spying. He was in solitary confinement in a Russian prison for eighteen months, and nearly went insane. In fact he wrote a book about his experiences of how he won his battle against insanity. He found the effects of the close regime frightening. If one considers his eighteen months in comparison to a life sentence with a recommendation of a minimum of thirty years, one will get some idea of what I and others are up against.

The public in general have got a wrong impression of my brother Ron. He can be very articulate and is a kind person in many ways, as he has proved in recent years. He has done a lot for charities which has not been advertised. My other brother Charlie keeps me happy with regular visits.

slang

During my stay at the hospital in Parkhurst I can recall some strange experiences. One day I was walking along with a friend of mine when I noticed him go white in the face, then he just walked away from me and butted a window in. Which makes me think when some people write to me and complain that it has been raining and I wonder how they would react under similar pressures.

Dr Cooper and his staff at the hospital have always been good to me, so I have no reason for complaint. All these memories are dear to mind because I have a retentive memory bank. My friends call me 'Scorpio'. All scorpions are supposed to have good memories.

Apart from the trouble caused by my illness some time back, I have not had any other real problems. I am a stable person with a calm personality. I have studied for mental progress over the years and have also kept physically fit by different methods of training.

I get along well with the inmates and staff at this prison, which makes my life more bearable.

Prison life has given me a good insight into human nature. I have mixed with all the notorious criminals in the country: Harry Roberts, the police killer, who adores his mother; I watched John Duddy die from the effects of a stroke. I have seen the pathetic ways of John Straffen the baby killer, and was aware of the evil eyes of Brady, the Moors murderer.

I am very happy in the main prison. How can I not be happy, alongside Charlie and Ron. Since beating paranoia and realising I have many friends, I feel the grass looks greener, the sun shines brighter, and people seem much nicer. Looking back over the years reminds me of an old proverb: 'A thousand years have passed by since yesterday.'

Parkhurst Prison, 1983.

COCKNEY

slang

*Dedicated to my father, Charles David Kray,
known to all his friends as 'Charlie'*

The origins of East End slang can be traced back to the sixteenth century.

It was first recorded by a Kentish gentleman, Thomas Harman, in his *Caveat* or *Warning*, published in 1566. The language of London had recently been affected by the coming of the Gypsies in 1530.

Slang (which then meant unconventional and unaccepted speech) was used mainly by soldiers and sailors, and as the latter docked in the Port of London, they spread their own professional idioms through the city, enriched by foreign importations they had picked up on their travels. But the slang which most interested Thomas Harman was 'cant' or thieves' slang.

The following are some of the terms which he recorded that have survived to the present day:

'nab' (later 'nob')	the head
'duds'	clothes
'boose' or 'booze'	drink
'stow you' (later 'stow it')	hold your peace
'niggle'	to have to do with a woman carnally
'cofe' (later 'cove' or 'coe')	man, fellow, chap
'prig'	to ride

In Elizabethan and Jacobean times, slang was given literary respectability by the great dramatists of the period – Shakespeare, Ben Jonson, Dekker, Middleton, Beaumont and Fletcher – who incorporated it in their plays.

In the nineteenth century, the poet Thomas Moore popularised 'cant' in his operatic sketch *Tom and Jerry* (1821), while the novelists – Dickens, Scott, Disraeli, Bulwer Lytton, Harrison Ainsworth – enlivened their stories with the then fashionable 'glorification of the underworld'. In these books, the Cockney characters transpose 'v' and 'w' (pronouncing 'veal' as 'weal' and 'wine' as 'vine') but this of course is no longer true today. The reason for the change is that during the huge influx of refugees to the East End at the end of the nineteenth century the European immigrants used the Germanic 'v' instead of the English 'w' (because they were accustomed to it and irrespective of any Cockney habit of speech) and laid so much stress on the sound that native East Enders actually went out of their way to avoid it.

Professor Ernest Weekley has written: 'Of all those historic dialects which distinguish to a greater or lesser degree the speech of most Englishmen, none is of such interest as Cockney, that noble blend of Mercian, Kentish and East Anglian, which, written by Chaucer, printed by Caxton, spoken by Spenser and Milton, and surviving in the mouths of Sam

Weller and Mrs Gamp, has, in modified form and with an artificial pronunciation, given us the literary English of the present day.'

The term 'Cockney' originally meant something to eat, then a spoilt child, then a milksop, then a pampered citizen, and finally in the sixteenth century, a Londoner. Cockney speech further developed in the nineteenth century, compounding the older London 'vulgar tongue' with structures and traditions carried into London by Irish, Jewish and other European immigrants. There was also a great influx to the East End from Kent and Essex in the nineteenth century, and a significant contingent from Middlesex, Surrey and the East Midlands, all of which influenced the dialect of the district.

Being a major trading centre, London has always been a linguistic crossroads: speech habits south of the Thames derive from Kentish sources, and that spoken north of the river is a variety of the Midland (or Mercian) dialect with an East Anglian and Essex flavour. The steady influx of families to London in the latter half of the nineteenth century fostered the organic growth of the city's dialect and slang. From about 1860, it was spread to the East End by costermongers whose speech was a mixture of back slang, cant and Romany borrowings: the East Enders adopted their terms for money, goods and people. Overcrowding, which caused intermingling, accelerated the rate at which these terms caught on.

Another vital influence on East End slang came from Yiddish idioms and patterns of speech. In 1753 there were only 10,000 British Jews, but by 1851 the number had risen to 35,000, of whom about 18,000 lived in London, mainly in the East End. Between 1881 and 1901, 40,000 Jews from Eastern Europe settled in Stepney alone. As a result of this influx, the population of Stepney during this period increased greatly, while the population of London as a whole increased by only 7.3%.

After the assassination of the Tsar Alexander II in 1881, and the ensuing expulsion laws, there was a steady immigration of Russian Jewish refugees into the East End of London. They spread beyond the confines of Aldgate and Commercial Street towards Brick Lane and into Mile End and Bethnal Green and down as far as Cable Street. In 1884, almost 30,000 Russo-Polish Jews lived in the East End. During the peak immigration at the end of the nineteenth century the number of new aliens averaged about 4,000 a year, and most of these settled in or around East London.

Visitors to the East End at this period were appalled by the conditions that they found there. A young Anglo-German writer, J. M. Mackay, wrote in 1891 about the streets of Whitechapel: 'The East End of London is a hell of poverty. Like an enormous black, giant kraken, the poverty of London lies there in lurking silence and encircles with its mighty tentacles the life and wealth of the City and of the West End . . .' If Mackay were to return to those streets today, he would not describe them in quite the same way, but the East End of London is still overcrowded. In Tower Hamlets alone there is a population of 20,000 Sikhs, Pakistanis and Bengalis. Since white and Asian children are educated together, the latter learn Cockney English, which is in turn picked up by their parents.

At the same time East End slang, which still retains echoes of the ancient idioms noted by Thomas Harman in 1566, is enriched by speech patterns from Urdu, Tamil and Bengali, as it was by Romany and Yiddish in the more recent past.

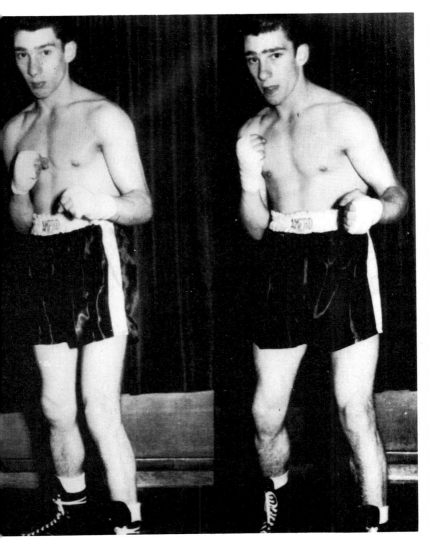

When this picture was taken, Reg (right) and Ron were Britain's only professional boxing twins. Both lightweights, they fought one another three times during amateur days – Ron winning twice – and they collected over 100 trophies between them. Ron had six professional fights, lost one and drew one; Reg had seven pro fights and won all of them.

Slang

Apples and pears: Stairs.
Ascot races: Braces.
Adam and Eve it: Believe it.
At the jump up: Stealing from lorries.
At the wheel: Driver.
At the flat: Flat racing.
Airy: Ventilator.
Aristotle: Bottle.
A stretch: One year.
'Arf a stretch: Six months.
Almond rocks: Socks.
Airs and graces: Braces.
Apple fritter: Bitter.
April Fools: Football pools.
Artful Dodger: Lodger.

Bad un: Bad person.
Bob Hope: Dope, Soap.
Brown bread: Dead.
Box of toys: Noise.
Bo Peep: Sleep.
Burglar: Cell searcher.
Bible puncher: Religious fanatic.
Berk or mug: Stupid.
Beak: Judge.
Brass: Prostitute.
Bird: Prison.
Birds: Females.
Boob: Prison.
Bottle: Courage.
Broad: Woman.

Blade: Knife.
Breaker: Car dismantler.
Bluey: Lead.
Bluey: £5 note.
Boozer: Pub.
Butcher's hook: Look.
Ball of chalk: Walk.
Bubble and squeak: Greek.
Bread and honey: Money.
Boracic lint: Skint . . . no money.
Bird lime: Time.
Bunsen burner: Earner.
Barnet Fair: Hair.
Boat race: Face.
Blagger: Robber.
Bugle: Nose.

Corned beef: Chief.
Chopper man: Hired assassin.
Currant bun: Sun.
Cosser: Police.
Chokey or block: Solitary confinement.
Con: Convict.
Chavy: Child.
Cushty mush: All's well, mate.
Choppers: Teeth.
Cadie: Hat.
Carpet: Three months.
Collar felt: Caught by police.
Chinas: Pals.
Chip: Shilling.

Reg and Frances on their wedding day.

Slang

China plate: Mate.
Cherry hog: Dog.
Chiv: Knife.
Carzey: Toilet.

Dick: Detective.
Daisy roots: Boots.
Dog and bone: Phone.
Ding dong: Sing song.
Digging the grave: Shave.
Duchess of Fife: Wife.
Dicky dirt: Shirt.
Date and plum: Bum.
Diamond: Compliment.
Dipping: Picking pockets.
Duff: No good.
Didloe or div: Insane.
Drop of parnie: Rain.
Darby Kelly: Belly.
Drum: Flat.
Drumming: Stealing from flats.
Daily Mail: Tail.
Duck and dive: Hide.
Dunlop tyre: Liar.
Dope: Drugs.

Earwig: To listen.
East and west: Vest.
Earner: Easy money.
Eighteen pence: Sense.

Fairy: Homosexual.
Frog and toad: Road.

Front-wheel skid: Yid.
Four by two: Jew.
Filbert gin: Chin.
Fog rocket: Small pocket.
Fog watch: Pocket watch.
Firm: Gang.
Fence: Receiver of stolen goods.
Frying pan: Old man.

Gavas: Police
Grass: Cannabis.
Grass: Informer.
Glimmer: Torch.
Groin: Ring.
Give a coating: Telling off.
Gunneff: Villain.
Good un: Good person.
Graft: Work.
Gregory Peck: Neck.
German bands: Hands.
Grasshopper: Copper.
Gaff: Home.
Gutted: Disappointed.

Had a tickle: Stole some money.
Hoister: Shop lifter.
Hooked him: Hit him.
Have it away: Escape.
Hairy ape: Rape.
Holy Ghost: Toast.
Harry Dash: Flash.
Hampstead Heath: Teeth.

Slang

Handle: Name.
Hebe: Jew.

Ivories: Teeth.
Ivories: Piano.
I suppose: Nose.
Iffy: Dodgy, no good.
Inside: In prison.
Isle of Wight: Light.
Ice: Diamonds.
Ice cream: Mug.
Itch and scratch: Match.

Jacks alive: Five.
Jam jar: Car.
Jekyll: Lives off immoral earnings. Snide.
Jam roll: Parole.
Jack Horner: Corner.
Jockey's whip: Chips.
Jar: Synthetic diamond.
Jimmie Riddle: Piddle.
Joey: Parcel.
Jam tart: Heart.
Joanna: Piano.
Jack and Jill: Till.
Jackanory: Story, lie.
Jem Mace: Face.
Jell: Go.
Jenny Linda: Window.
Jimmy O'Goblin: Sovereign.
Joe Brown: Town.
Joe Hook: Crook.

Kite: Forged cheque.
Kippers: Slippers.
Kosher: Trusted.
Knock back: Refusal.
Kettle: Watch.
Kangaroo: Jew.
Kate: Army.

Local: Pub.
Long firm: Fraud.
Loaf of bread: Head.
Lagging: Three years.
Linen draper: Paper.
Legged it: Ran away.
Lobster and crab: Cab.
Lrig: Girl.
Lilley and Skinner: Dinner.
Longer and linger: Finger.
Loop the loop: Soup.
Lord Lovel: Shovel.

Mince pies: Eyes.
Man on the moon: Spoon.
Mitts: Hands.
Manor: Area.
Mumble brock: Good luck.
Mutton Jeff: Deaf.
Make one: Do something.
Mars bar: Scar.
Mangles and wringers: Fingers.
Mulla: Kill.

slang

Moody: To kid someone.
Mother of pearl: Girl.

Nonce: Sex offender.
Nelson Riddle: Fiddle.
Nitto: Keep quiet.
Nevis: Seven years.
North 'n' south: Mouth.
Nancy Lee: Flea.
Nap and double: Trouble.
Needle: Annoy.
Night and day: Play.
Nick: Prison.
Noah's Ark: Lark.

On one: Out thieving.
On the knocker: Hawking.
Oxford scholar: Dollar.
On the house: Free.
Oats and barley: Charlie.
On your tod: On your own.
Oyzens: Trousers.
Old lady: Wife.
Old Bill: Police.

Pickey: Gypsy.
Porridge: Sentence.
Paraffin lamp: Tramp.
Plates of meat: Feet.
Peter: Cell, safe.
Peter man: Safe-blower.
Pension: Easy money.
Pork pies: Eyes.

Pen and ink: Stink.
Pig's ear: Beer.
Put the leather in: Kicked someone.
Poke: Money.
Pulling a stroke: Deceiving someone.
Plot: Area.
Pat Malone: Alone.
Pimple and blotch: Scotch.
Pouf: Homosexual.

QE: Going Queen's evidence.
Queenie: Mother or wife.
Quack: Doctor.

Readies: Money.
Railings: Teeth.
Ruck: To cause trouble.
Rosie Lee: Tea.
Rip offs: Conned.
Raspberry ripple: Cripple.
Red: Gold.
Ringing: Stealing cars.
Ringer: Stolen car.
Ruby Murray: Curry.
Rabbit and pork: Talk.
Richard the Third: Bird.
Rattler: Train.
Robin Hood: Good.
Rub a dub dub: Night club.
Rub down: Search.
Rozzer: Police.

Slang

Stand at ease: Cheese
SP: Starting price.
Snout: Tobacco.
Scotch pegs: Legs.
Strides: Trousers.
Skin and blister: Sister.
Skint: Got no money.
Soapy: Dirty person.
Snouters: Tobacconists.
Spade: Negro.
Sticks: Rural areas.
Scratch: Money.
Slippery Sid: Yid.
Smoke: London.
Slag: Contemptible person.
Screw: Prison officer.
Stir crazy: Institutionalised.
Sky rocket: Pocket.
Smother: Overcoat.
Speeler: Gambling club.
Salmon and trout: Snout.
Sinbad the sailor: Tailor.
Snide: False.
On spec: Chance.
Steam tug: Mug.
Stewed prune: Tune.
Stone ginger: A certainty.
Stir: Prison.
Swear and cuss: Bus.

Tea leaf: Thief.
Tool: Weapon.
Top jolly: Leader.

To moonlight: Leave overnight.
Tackle: Gold chain.
Titfer tat: Hat.
Turtle doves: Gloves.
Tomfoolery: Jewellery.
Trouble and strife: Wife.
Taiters mould: Cold.
Tickle: Good result, thieving.
Tin tack: Sack.
Tommy Tucker: Sucker.
Trick cyclist: Psychiatrist.

Uncle Ned: Bed.
Up front: Leader.
Uncle's: Pawn shop.

Vera Lynn: Gin.
Vassle: Police.

Wally: Idiot.
Whistle and flute: Suit.
Willy nilly: Silly.
Weeping willow: Pillow.
Weigh in: To give.
Westminster Abbey: Shabby.
Wilkie Bards: Cards.
Wrap it up: To tie up.

Yobbo: Thug.
Yoch: Christian.
Yid: Jew.

PHRASES

Getting stroppy: Getting cheeky.

Not the full ticket: A bit stupid.

To get a rec: Recommended sentence.

The three-card trick: Con trick.

To case a joint: To sum a place up.

At the whizz: Pickpocketing.

Cop for his boat and blow: Look at his face and go.

He's at the jack and danny so blank him: He's kidding, so ignore him.

Nit, it's a cosser: Keep quiet, it's a policeman.

Have a Joe Blake: Have a steak.

Not a bad judge: A good judge of character.

Get on the rattler: Get on the train.

To read and write: To have a fight.

The Sweeney Todd: The Flying Squad.

At the toss: Tossing a coin.

Plenty on top: Very brainy.

On the out: Outside the prison.

A head banger: A nut case.

To be blocked: To be stopped.

Had the manor sewn up: Had the area under control.

Behind the door: In your cell.

On your bottle: On your tail.

At the hurry up: To take one out of stride.

Swallows it: Backed down.

Get a rhubarb: A sub from your wages.

Get the wind up: To be tense.

A saucepan lid: A Yid, Jew.

The Green: Bethnal Green.

Do a cherry: To blush.

A stiff: Illegal letter.

slang

He goes up: Goes to court.
To cop for it: To get hold of.
At the flannel: To talk a load of rubbish.
Have a rabbit: Have a conversation.
One of the old school: One of the lads.
Near the mark: Near the truth.
To be slommory: To be sloppy.
Too much gate: Too much mouth.
Out with the bag: Hawking for old clothes.

Ron with Lord Boothby, his friend and business associate.

AMERICAN slang

PREFACE

By Andrew Ray

It gives me great pleasure to write this preface to the book on American slang written by my friend Reg Kray.

I come from a show business family (my father was Ted Ray, the well-known British comedian from Liverpool, and my mother was one of Cochrane's original Young Ladies from Fulham). Rhyming slang was very much in use at home from as long ago as I can remember. Perhaps the reason for this was that by tradition show business people were part of a minority group, and in the old days rather frowned upon by society as a whole. Like every minority group they would find a way of protecting themselves, and to have their own 'language' was one of them. Perhaps this is how 'back slang' and 'rhyming slang' grew up in the various cultures around the world.

I feel that this book will be most instructive and informative for all who read it and can only help to build bridges between society at large and minority groups around the world who have always for one reason or another felt outsiders.

Andrew Ray's show business background encouraged his acting and he entered films in the title role of *The Mudlark*, which was the Royal Command Performance film for 1950. From this role Andrew was given a seven-year contract by 20th Century-Fox. Many films followed such as *The Yellow Balloon*, *Woman in a Dressing Gown*, *Escapade*, *Gideon's Day*, *Prize of Gold* and more recently *Rough Cut* (with Burt Reynolds and David Niven), and *The Bunker* (a movie about the last days of Hitler, filmed entirely on location in Paris).

Andrew has also starred in many West End plays too numerous to mention here, but they include *Flowering Cherry* which co-starred Sir Ralph Richardson, and *Crown Matrimonial* in which he played the role of George VI. Andrew has also appeared on Broadway, repeating his London success in *Flowering Cherry* and appearing in Joan Littlewood's production of *A Taste of Honey* (for which Andrew won the best actor on Broadway award). There have been many TV appearances as well.

Slang

F O R E W O R D

By Reg Kray

Slang consists of words and phrases in common colloquial use, but generally considered in some or all of their sense to be outside of standard English.

Hoboes travelling from city and towns throughout the United States helped to bring about a mixture of words that resulted in slang. These hoboes travelled mostly by the freight trains.

Also all the different ethnic groups and refugees from all over the world brought to play different phrases and words, as they too travelled the country.

Sicilian, Polish, Jewish, Italian and Puerto Rican settlers all unconsciously aided the usage of slang, hence its wide popularity.

Different fraternities and uniformed groups also find a common bond of comfort from the use of slang, to protect and unite them against outsiders.

I hope this book will give you pleasure.

slang

Abe's Cabe: A five-dollar bill.

A-Bomb: An exceptionally fast hot rod car.

AC-DC: Bisexual.

Ace: A one-dollar bill.

Ace-Deuce: Three or trey of playing cards.

Ace in the hole: Any important fact.

Ace of spades (derog.): Negro.

Across, get: To explain successfully.

Action: Gambling activity, especially fast play for high stakes.

Adam and Eve on a raft: Bacon and eggs.

Adobe dollar: A Mexican peso.

African dominoes: Dice.

African golf: African dominoes.

Agony pipe: A clarinet.

Air: To jilt.

Air, take the: To go away.

Air (one's) belly: To vomit.

Airedale: An ugly, ill-mannered, uncouth, or boring man or youth.

Air-log: An altimeter.

Air out: 1. To leave, to flee. 2. To stroll, to saunter.

Altar kocker: Ass kisser.

Akey okey: OK, all right.

Alarm clock: A chaperone.

Albert: A watch chain, especially a gold one.

Alfalfa: 1. Hay. 2. Money. 3. Smoking tobacco.

Alfred: Al.

Alibi Ike: One who habitually makes excuses.

Alkali: 1. Whisky. 2. Coffee.

Alky, Alki, Alchy: Alcohol, alcoholic.

All: Everyone or everything, anything or anyone.

Alley apple: A piece of horse manure.

Alligator: A Mississippi River keelboat sailor.

Alligator bait: A Negro.

All in: Exhausted, tired.

All of a doodah: Completely or suddenly confused.

All reet, all reat, all root: All right.

All shook, all shook up: All excited, stimulated, disturbed, upset.

All six, hit on: To do well.

All the way: Completely, for all time, without reservation.

All to the mustard: OK, all right.

All wasted: All wrong.

Altogether in the birthday suit: Naked.

Alyo: A routine task.

Am: An amateur performer.

Ambish: Ambition, aggressiveness.

Ameche: A telephone.

Americano: An American.

Ammo: Ammunition of all kinds.

Ammonia: Carbonated water.

Amp: An ampere.

Amy-John: A female homosexual.

Angel: One who donates money to a politician's campaign fund.

Angel factory: A theological seminary.

Angel food: Mission-house preaching.

Ankle: To walk, to amble.

Annie, Annie Oakley: A meal ticket especially one issued to circus performers.

Anti: One who is not in favour of any specific plan or action.

Any, get: Sexual intercourse.

Anyhoo: Anyhow.

A-1, A-One: Any excellent or first-rate person or thing.

Ape (derog.): A Negro.

Apple: A saddle horn.

Apple butter: Smooth talk.

Apple-pie: Neat and tidy.

Apple-head: A stupid person.

Apron: A bartender.

Aqua: Water.

Aquarium: A Roman Catholic rectory.

Arab: Any wild-looking person.

Arizona: Buttermilk.

Arkansas lizard: A louse.

Arkansas toothpick: Any hunting knife when used for fighting.

Armstrong heater(s): The arm(s) of one's sweetheart.

Army chicken: Beans and frankfurters.

Army strawberries: Prunes.

Around the world: To kiss all over one's lover's body.

Arrowhead: A wallflower, an unpopular girl.

Art: Photographs of wanted criminals.

Arthur Duffy, take it on the: To run away fast.

B.A.: Bare-assed.

Babe: A girl or woman of any age.

Baby doll: A pretty girl.

Baby kisser: A politician.

Backasswords: Ass backwards.

Back talk: Impudent talk.

Back up: To support.

Slang

Badge bandit: A motorcycle policeman.
Ball and chain: One's wife.
Balmy: Drunk.
Bam: To strike or hit.
Bandhouse: A prison.
Bang to rights: Caught on the job.
Bark: 1. Money. 2. Human skin.
Beard: An intellectual person.
Beat the drum: Talk too much.
Bed house: A brothel.
Beef: A complaint.
Beef-squad: A gang of tough men employed for violent purposes.
Beekie: Any nosey person.
Beezer: Any person's nose.
Biddy: An Irish servant girl.
Biff: A blow with the fist.
The Big Pond: The Atlantic Ocean.
Blind pig: A speakeasy.
Boffo: A dollar.
Boff: To hit.
Bog-hopper: An Irishman.
Boil out: To leave quickly.
Bolo: An unskilled rifleman.
Boog: To dance.
Boobs: The breasts.
Boogie-woogie: Secondary syphilis.

Booze: Any type of liquor.
Boozed up: Drunk.
Booter: Bootlegger.
Bozo: A man.
Brat: To baby-sit.
Brass tacks: The essential facts.
Buck: A dollar.

C: A hundred dollars.
Cab: The cockpit of a plane.
Cabin girl: A chambermaid.
Cake cutter: One who short changes.
Cake eater: A ladies' man.
Call back: A request to return.
Candy: Cocaine.
Canoe: To have sexual intercourse.
Caper juice: Whisky.
Cartwheel: A silver dollar.
Catholic: Pickpocket.
Cat lick: A Catholic.
CC pills: Laxative pills of any kind.
Chain man: A watch thief.
Cheap John: Unknown.
Chev: Knife.
Chic sale: An outdoor toilet.
Chinny: Talkative.
Chisel: To cheat someone.
Chow down: To eat a meal.
Chow hall: An eating place.
Chub: A Texan.

Slang

Chug wagon: A car.
Clean: Innocent of carrying illegal goods.
Clip joint: A place of public entertainment.
Clobber: Clothing.
Close up: To stop talking.
Clout: To hit someone.
Clunkhead: A stupid person.
Coalhole: A prison cell.
Coffee bag: Any pocket.
Cold meat: A dead person.
Colly: To understand.
Comeback: A recovery of health.
Conk: The head.
Con man: A confidence man.
Coo coo: Unconscious.
Cop: A policeman.

D: Detective.
DA: Drug addict.
Daily mail: Ship under sail.
Daisy: A safe-breaking tool.
Damper: A light snack.
Dancers: Stairs.
Darb: Money.
Darby roll: Parole.
Dead letter: A corpse.
Dead picker: A robber or drunk.
Deck: As pack of cards.

Decko: Watch, guard.
Dial: Face.
Dimmer: A dime.
Diving: Pickpocketry.
Do a crib: To rob a house.
Do time: Serve a prison sentence.
Doe: An infant.
Dope head: A drug addict.

Eagle eye: A detective.
Earth bath: A grave.
East and south: Mouth.
Eat a fig: To commit burglary.
Edge: To escape, make off.
Elephant ears: A policeman.
Ellsway: Yes or rather.
Expand one's chest: To be self-assured.
Ex con: A former convict.
Eye doctor: Tramp or beggar.
Eye water: Gin.
Equalizer: A gun.
Erase: To kill.
Enforcer: Hard-boiled member of a mob.

Face lace: Whiskers.
Fairy: Opium smoker.
Fag factory: A homosexual brothel.
Fair trade: Smuggling.

Fakir: A circus worker.

Fakus Mr: A store detective.

Fence: Receiver of stolen goods.

Ferry: A prostitute.

Fiddle and flute: A suit.

Filcher: A petty thief.

Fine as silk: In good condition.

Finger's end: A ten per cent share out.

Fiver: Five years' imprisonment.

Flash gill: Member of the underworld.

Flat tyre: An impotent man.

Flicker: A glass.

Fly my kite: Light.

Flying cat: An owl.

Foiler: A pickpocket.

Fumbles: Gloves.

Fuzzy: A policeman.

G: One thousand dollars.

G man: A government agent.

Gad: Shirt.

Gaff: Dwelling.

Gagers: Eyes.

Gallies: A pair of boots.

Galway: A Catholic priest.

Game pullet: A whore.

Gammoning cove: A juvenile thief.

Gammy: Bad.

Garden hop: To betray.

Gas hotel: A garage.

Gash: The mouth.

Garters: Leg irons.

Geblakker: Tipsy.

Geco: A good friend.

German flutes: Boots.

Gerver: A safe-blower.

Gig: To look.

Glim star: A finger ring.

God's medicine: Morphine.

Gondola: An open railway-car.

Grand: A thousand dollars.

Grease: To bribe.

Griddeler: One who busks for a living.

Gull: A simpleton.

Gyppo: A sub-contractor.

H: Heroin.

Habit: A craving for drugs.

Hackie: Taxi man.

Half G: Five-hundred dollars.

Hang out: One's home.

Handy wagon: Police wagon.

Hangman's Day: Friday.

Haul in: To arrest.

Havil: Sheep.

Hawker: A private detective.

Heater: A firearm.

Heap: A car.

Hell's kitchen: A foundry.

Hickory dock: A clock.

Slang

High bloke: A well-dressed fellow.
High tober: Potter.
High toby: A highwayman.
Hippy: Insane.
Hook a button: Button.

I declare: A chair.
Ice: Prison sentence.
Ice box: Prison at Dannemora.
Iced: In jail.
I'm afloat: Boat.
Inching: Encroaching.
Indoway: Window.
Innocent: A corpse.
Inky smudge: A judge.
Irish buggy: A wheelbarrow.
Irish lasses: Glasses.
Irish turkey: Corned beef and cabbage.
Ironed: In handcuffs.
Iron doublet: Prison.
Itchland: Scotland.
Ivories: Teeth.
Isaac: A pawnbroker.

JB: A stetson.
Jab joint: A dope den.
Jabber: A prize fighter.
Jack: To lock a door.
Jack Ketch: A hangman.
Jacksie: Brothel.

Jackey: Gin.
Jade: A long term of imprisonment.
Jail bird: A prisoner.
Jamoke: Coffee.
Jane: A sovereign.
Jasker: A seal on a letter.
Jaum: To discover.
Jawbone: Credit.
Jerry: To injure.
Jink: Money.
Jit: A nickel.
John: A man.
Joiner: One who builds a mob.
Jorem: Jug.
Juggins: Food handed out to a beggar.
Ju-ju: Drugged cigarette.

K: Homosexual.
KC: Kansas City.
KO'd: Knocked out.
Keep: A boy.
Kelp: To help a person.
Kelly Ned: The head.
Ken burster: A housebreaker or burglar.
Kewpie: An infant.
Kick in: To die.
Kid glove worker: A criminal clerk.
Kidder: A middle-man.

Slang

Kneipe: A speakeasy.
Knecker: A low cheat.
Knob: The head.
Knockover: A kidnapping.
Knock-off gee: A paid killer.
Kroo: A Negro.
Krupp: A large revolver.
Kuter: 25 cents.

Label: To hit or strike.
Lace: To thrash.
Lace: Without money.
Lag-boy: A man that has been in prison.
Lagging-cove: A magistrate.
Lain: A sucker.
Land doper: A vagabond.
Larkin: A girl.
Latch: A breast-pin.
Lawaaiwater: Strong liquor.
Lay: Milk.
Lay in: To remain in one's cell and not go to work.
Lay out: To kill a person.
Leaf: A purse.
Lean and fat: Hat.
Legaler: A barrister.
Lent: 'Japanese fibrous morphine'.
Lettuce: Paper money.
Lightning: Gin.
Limey: An Englishman.

Lobster: A soldier.
Long-bit or short-bit: Long sentence or short sentence.

M: Morphine.
Mabber: A cab-driver.
Mace: To cheat.
Mack: A pimp.
Maidstone jailer: A tailor.
Make: A halfpenny.
Makins: Cigarette, tobacco and papers.
Mang: To speak or talk.
Mary Warner: A marijuana cigarette.
Mashed T-bones: Hamburger.
Meat: Women.
Mickey Finn: A 'double' drink of any spirit.
Mitre: A hat.
Mollisher: A woman.
Montra: A watch.
Monnicker: Name.
Mope: To talk away.
Mousing: Petty theft.
Mug-show: Confrontation with witnesses.
Muns: To kiss.
Murk: Coffee.
My nabs: Myself.
Myrnionger: A newly arrived convict.

NQA: No questions will be asked.
Nab the bib: To weep.
Nabs: A person of either sex.
Nack: A horse.
Nail: To arrest.
Natty: Smartly dressed.
Near and far: A bar.
Nib: The human mouth.
Newgale: The inside vest pocket.
Nix: Nothing.
Nipping jig: The gallows.
Nob for: To feel for.
Noll: A wig.
Noisy pegs: A pair of boots.
Nursery: A reform school.

Occupy: To wear.
OZ: A ration of narcotics.
Office: To warn.
Oh by heck: The neck.
Old Mr Gory: A piece of gold.
One-two-three and splash: A dish frequently served in prison.
Onicker prostitute: Whore.
One-spot: A prison term for one year.
Onion: A seal.
Ostler: A house thief.
Ostrich: A lady.
Outing dues: A hanging.

Over-all: A coat.
Over the stile: Go to trial.
Owner: A pimp.

PA: American tramps.
PI: Pimp.
Pack in: To finish a sentence.
Pad borrower: A horse thief.
Padder: A highway robber.
Paddy print: A finger print.
Pal: A friend.
Palm: Cheat.
Pan: To defame.
Panneller: A panel thief.
Panzy: A burglar.
Parkey: A trial.
Patter: To talk.
Pawned: Imprisoned.
Pete, Peteman: A strong-box or safe-blower.
Ped: A basket.
Pen: Prison.
Pedigree: A criminal's police record.
Pete dice: False dice.
Phunt: One pound sterling.
Picket hatch: A brothel.
Pigeon: A dupe.
Pipe: A detective.
Pineapple: To bomb.
Pinyon: Opium.
Pint pot: A drunkard.
Place: A hiding place.

Slang

Poke-out: A lunch.
Poke: To pick pockets.
Pork: A corpse.
Punce: A male homosexual.
Pull the pin: To quit work.

Quack: To inform the police.
Quail: An old maid.
Queen's bus: A prison van.
Quandong: A prostitute.
Queer bit: Bad money.
Queer looking money: Forged money.
Queer-Ken Hall: Prison.
Queck: Look out.
Queter: A quarter-dollar.
Quids: Money.
Quod-cove: A prison warder.
Quota: Snack, share, or part.

RO: Run out.
Racket: An underworld trick or means of livelihood.
Radiator: A large diamond.
Rafe: A pawnbrokers duplicate.
Rag shop: A bank.
Railroad: To convict.
Rails: A sentence of imprisonment.
Rake: A portion.
Ramble: An automobile.
Range: A tier or gallery in prison.

Rap: To commit perjury, police charge.
Rasher wagon: A frying pan.
Rattlers: The railway.
Record: Police record.
Red-lighter: A prostitute.
Red scatter: A brothel.
Red-stuff: Gold jewellery.
Respun: To steal.
Ribbin: Money.
Righty: Tramp.
Riot-gun: A sawn-off shotgun.
River pirates: River thieves.
Rod: A revolver.
Rod-man, rod toter: A gunman.
Rowdy: Money.

SA: State Attorney.
Sack diver: A pickpocket.
Sad: A sadistic sexual pervert.
Saddle and bridle: An opium smoker's kit.
Salmon: An altar.
Sago: Money.
Saltee: One or one penny.
Salvation rancher: A missioner.
Sand: Moist sugar.
Sappy: Simple.
Sarbot: An informer.
Sawbuckle: A ten-dollar bill.
Sausage: A small coin.

Ron with Tony Bennett.

Slang

Scaler: A burglar.
Scarlet pips: Lips.
Schooling: A low gambling party.
Scoot: To run.
Scragg's hotel: A workhouse.
Scrapper: Fighter.
Scraper: Barber.
Scratch: Any piece of writing.
Screeve model: Forgery.
Scriff: To betray.
Scurf: Arrested.
Send-in: Note.
Shackles: Soup.

Tab: To name.
Tack: To beg food.
Tail-buzzer: A pickpocket.
Tail pit: Side pocket of coat.
Take-beef: To run away.
Tan: To beat up.
Talent: Professional criminals.
Tank: To drink.
Taxi: A sentence of between five and fifteen years.
Tease: A slave at work.
Tenner: A sentence of ten years' imprisonment.
Thimble: A watch.
Thing: A robbery.
Third rail: 1. Whisky. 2. Tramps.
Throw-down: Betray.

Throw-off: A front.
Thud: To walk.
Ticklers: Ribs.
Tickety boo: The deputy governor.
Tin throne: A water-closet in the cell.
Tin ear: To eavesdrop.
Timbers: Pencils.
Ting-a-ling: Finger ring.
Tin-opener: A safe robber's instrument applied to the back of the safe.
Tip-off: To inform upon.
Tip-up: To die.
Tit-for-tat: Hat.
Titlark: A spectator or witness.

Uckersay: A dupe.
Udjay: A jail.
Under beneaths: Teeth.
Undercover: Safe from the police.
Underground kite: Illicit letter.
Under shell: Waistcoat.
Unmugged: The police have no photos of you.
Up for: Up for trial.
Unslour: To unlock.
Uphills: False dice.
Upstairs: The inside breast pocket.

Usher: Yes.

V: Five dollars.
Vag: Vagrant, to run.
Valentine: One year in prison.
Vamp: To pawn.
Vardo: To look.
Varment: Vermin.
Venite: Come.
Very best: The chest.
Vinegar boy: A passer of worthless cheques, forger.
Viper: An informer to the police.
Vodeodo: Money.
Voker: To speak.

Waffle iron: The electric chair.
Wall: Resistance.
Waif: A hobo, tramp that sleeps in jail.
Walk the plank: Identification parade.
Wall City: San Quentin prison.
Waller: A policeman.
Wattles: Ears.
Watcher: A look-out man.
Wax-zucker: A bribe.
Wear the broad arrow: To be a convict.
Wedge feeder: A silver spoon.
Weigh off: Sentence passed.
Welcher: A twister.

Whacks: A prison sentence.
Whirl: A try, an attempt.
Whiddle: To divulge.
Whiff: To shoot.
White: Silver.
White-house: Jail.
White prop: A diamond pin.
Wide: Alert.
White super: A silver watch.
Windows: Spectacles.
Wimpy: A hamburger.
Wipe the clock: To halt.

X-Division: Swindlers, thieves.
X's Hall: The sessions house.
X-Ray: A 10,000-dollar bill.

Y: To double cross.
Yard hack: A prison guard.
Yeder: Everyone.
Yank: To arrest.
Yed: A Jew.
Yaffle: To purloin.
Yabo: A fool.
Yokel: A country-man.
Yellow cloak: A jealous husband.
Yike: An argument.
Yewman: A carpenter.
Yellow one: A gold watch.
Yegg: To beg.
Yen: Craving for opium.
Yell copper: Informer.

SLANG

Yoni: A woman.
Yunker: A country bumpkin.
Young horse: Roast beef.
York: A look.

Zabist: A policeman.
Zack: Six months' imprisonment.

Zulu: An immigrant car.
Zook: A worn out old prostitute.
Zol: A dagga cigarette.
Zex: A warning.
Ziff: A juvenile thief.
Zebra: Prison uniform.
Zib: A nincompoop.

CRIMINAL slang

AG: Acting Governor.

Aggro: Aggravation.

Bang up: To lock in a cell.

Bent: Crooked, illegal. Used chiefly of goods.

Bird: Bird-lime – time. Time of prison sentence.

Blags: Robberies by force.

Blister: A summons.

Bogy-waggon: Police car or black maria. A bogy-man was once a policeman and bogy is still sometimes used.

Book thrown: To have the book thrown at you is to be given the maximum sentence for the offence.

Bottle: He has no bottle means he has no firm foundation as a thief, he's not to be relied on. His bottle's gone.

Brass: Prostitute.

Bracelets: Handcuffs.

Brass nucks: Knuckle-dusters.

Brighton: Brighton Rock – the dock.

Bubble: To bubble and squeak – to squeak to the police.

Bint: Girl.

Ray with Johnnie Ray

Bory mush: Governor.

Bung: To pay, to bribe.

Burn the town: To exhaust the possibilities of a place for one's own racket.

Buzz: To distract someone's attention while his pocket is being picked. 'On the buzz', pickpocketing.

Bender: Suspended sentence.

Blue brick: Prison.

Cabbage: Paper money.

Cane: Jemmy.

Card-marking: Giving advice or instructions.

Carpet: Three months' imprisonment.

Case: 1. To look over or prospect a place for thieving. 2. 'Going case', taking a woman to bed.

China: China plate – mate.

Chisel: To swindle.

Chiv: Knife or razor (gypsy).

Clammed: Hungry, starved.

Clip: To steal a part of a thing, to take a cut of something.

Clobber: Clothes.

College: Prison. 'He is in college'. Formerly meant Newgate.

Con: 1. To work a confidence trick on. 2. A prisoner.

Conger: To conger eel – to squeal.

Corner: A share.

Cutters: Oxyacetylene tools.

Clip joint: Watered-down drinker.

Crow: Inform.

Dab: Finger prints.

Darbies: Handcuffs.

Didakais: Half-bred gypsies.

Diddies: Slang term for didakais.

Dish out: To sentence. A judge is said to 'love dishing it out'.

Dolly mixtures: Films.

Down to the old pals act: All free of charge.

Drag: The road.

Dragging: Working a swindle or thieving on the roads.

Dropsy: Money.

Drum: House.

Duck eggs: Irishmen.

Factory: Police station. 'The confession factory'.

Fish-and-tank: Bank.

Flimp: To cheat.

Flog: To sell.

Fork: A hand. 'To fork' is to shake hands, formerly to pickpocket.

Form: Previous imprisonment. 'He's got a lot of form.'

Fours: Fourth landing in a prison. 'He's on the fours.'

Front: Plenty of show.

Fanny: 1. A likely story. 2. A bird's pussy.

Figure six: Cockney style of male hairdressing.

Fadge: A farthing.

Gaff: House, shop, stall, site.

Gear: Stolen goods.

Geezer: Man – stranger.

Grass: 1. Grasshopper – copper. 2. A police informer.

German Band: Hand.

Hand on the collar: Arrest.

Holidays: Imprisonment. 'He's on his holidays.'

Hot cross bun: 'On the hot cross', on the run.

Half a bean: Half a guinea.

Jack: 1. 'On his Jack' or 'On his Jack Jones', on his own. 2. A farthing.

Jack Ketch: A stretch.

Jeremiah: Fire.

Law: 'The law' means among thieves 'the police'. 'The Law arrived' – the police arrived.

Leather: A kicking.

Lollipop or Lolli: A shop.

Lustpot: Sex maniac.

Lumbered: Tied up.

Laggin: Three years in prison.

Little smack: A ten-shilling note.

Manor: District. Used both of police districts and criminals' districts. 'He lives in my manor.'

Mark a card: See card-marking.

Monkey: £500.

Moosh: A man (gypsy).

Mort: A woman.

Needle: Anger. 'I got the raving needle', I was furious.

Newgates: Inside pockets.

Nick: Prison. To nick, to arrest.

Nicker: A pound.

Nine and thirty: Example of a punishment awarded by a prison governor. Nine days in punishment cells and thirty days' lost remission.

Slang

Nonces: Sex cases.
Nark: Police informer.
Ned: A guinea piece.
Nose turn: To turn QE (Queen's evidence).

Old Bill: The police.
Ounce: A crown (five shillings).
Oliver Twist: A fist, wrist.

Palone: A girl.
Pat: Pat Malone, alone.
Peter: A safe. Used also of a prison cell.
Peter-blower: Safe-blower.
Piece off: To square by giving a share.
Pitching: Selling at markets.
Powder: 'To take a powder', to disappear quickly.
Promised land: 'In promised land', living on false promises.
Parney: Rain.
Porridge: Time in prison.
Plate: Oral love-making.

Quack: Doctor.

Rabbit: To chatter.
Red: Gold.
Roll: To rob a man's person. 'He was rolling drunks.'

Rory: Rory O'Moore – door or floor.

Screw: A word of many meanings. To screw is to rob. A screwsman is a thief. A screw is a prison officer. Also to have sexual intercourse.
Six-and-eight: Straight.
Sky, sky-rocket: Pocket.
Snout: Tobacco, from the sign (touching the nose) used by convicts to ask for tobacco in the days of silent prisons.
Suss: Suspicious person.
Sterrika: Hard case.
Swagman: Dealer in cheap market goods and fairground prizes.
Spinning: Searching.
Scrubber: A rough-looking girl.
Speeler: Gambling den.
Stiff: Illegal note or letter.
Stoppo: Being chased by the law.
Speel, Spiel: Story.
Stooly: Police informer.
Slagging: Aggressive telling off.
Slags: Low-down, no principles.

Tea leaf: Thief.

Tickle: Theft. 'He had a nice tickle last week.'

Toberman: A man in charge of a market who lets pitches.

Tom, tomfoolery: Jewellery.

Top: To hang. The hangman used to be called the 'topping-cove'.

Top weight: Maximum of sentences.

Tub: A bus. 'He was working on the tubs', he was pickpocketing on the buses.

Turkey: 'On the turkey' or 'on the turkey-trot', on the trot, on the run.

Turtles: Turtle-doves – gloves.

Twirl: Key.

Threes: Third landing in a prison.

Turnover: Cell search.

Tearaway: Villain, good fighter.

Trumped up: Fabricated.

Twos: Second landing in prison.

Weed: 1. To take part of, to nibble at. 2. Dope.

Weigh off: To sentence.

Wank: One off the wrist.

Wooden plank: Yank, American.

Yocks: Eyes.

Reg Kray.

slang

PARANOIA

By Patsy Manning
Long Lartin Prison, 1981

A population full of paranoia is hidden in our long-term hells,
An illness that is forced upon the prisoner's mind, that breeds
   in the prison cells,
It brings a terrible fear to each of them who fall victim to its
   fearful grip,
A phantom paranoia sneaks upon them, and without warning,
   it's a nightmare trip,
Disordered reason captivates their minds and the pain is so
   hard to bear,
It's not a pain from a punch, or a tooth which aches, nor even
   a love affair,
It's a morbid fear and it frightens them to death, so they think
   everybody wants to kill,
The worst thing is you can't get away, you're for ever
   paranormal, and you're ill,
There's no escape because there's nowhere to go, paranoia's got
   a hold of you,
It gets a powerful grip upon a prisoner's mind and there's
   nothing in their world they can do,
Right here in Long Lartin prison I can see it everywhere, it will
   eventually drive all the men mad,
You can see them doing things like psychopaths do, and it's
   very, very, very, very sad.

S L A N G

by Patsy Manning

Slang *is this book written by Reggie Kray,*
To give information about what the words say.
The words are interesting if you know what they mean
But by the majority of people they have never been seen.
Sterrika *is Jewish and it means a hard case;*
Boat race *is rhyming slang, and that is your face;*
To a Romany gypsy a chiv *is a knife,*
If you don't want to be chived *run for your life.*
Now in India when it's raining they call that parney,
So we borrowed this from India as you can see.
We have words from the Arabs, like a girl is a bint,
And when you are brassic *that's when you're skint.*
To touch your nose in prison means you want a cigarette,
Because nosegay *in the old days was all the* burn *you'd get,*
And because silence was the rule and talking was out;
Tobacco barons in prisons called tobacco snout.
Grasshopper *is a copper: thus the word* grass,
Which brings us to the prostitute and she is a brass.
To understand Romany you must be able to chant the can,
A bory mush *is a governor and a* roy *is a gentleman.*
When a gypsy chy *goes out* duckering, *she will read the palm*
   of your hand;
While a Cockney spiv *in a London pub says, 'Give us your*
   German band.'
In Birmingham you are a yoe, *in London you are a* ya,
So in most of the towns in the British Isles you are a you *or a*
   yoe *or a* ya.
The more words you know the shrewder you are:
You will understand wide boys *who drink at the bar,*
You will understand grafters *who live on their wits,*
And most of the women will love you to bits.
The English are the Tommies, *the Germans are the* Hun,

Slang

*So slang is a language to speak, you know, because it's a lot of
    fun.*
Everyone knows the Americans are often referred to as Yanks,
But here in London town, my son, we call them wooden planks.
If they send you off to prison, you are choked, *'cos you're in
    the* blue brick,
*And if you don't understand slang in there, you have got to be
    really thick.*
So slang is a jargon that's useful to use:
It's used by the prisoners and heard by the screws.
Slang is spoken all over the world in every city you go:
It makes no difference where you are, it's always nice to know.
*If you hear slang spoken at the movies, or hear it spoken on
    TV,*
*And don't understand the dialogue, Reggie's book is the best
    book to see.*
So when you go on a journey, take Slang *along with you,*
And read it, and read it, all the way through.

THE LIFER'S CELL

A Poem dedicated to Reg Kray by Patsy Manning

There is no bus, he has no car.
He never ventures very far.
Locked in a small room called a cell.
Abode of the damned he knows it well.

Big enough to take one stride.
Small enough to destroy his mind.
After time it seems to grow.
It gets much bigger as years go.

The days get shorter day by day.
It seems his life will run away.
There is no bus, he has no car.
He never travels very far.

Time is short and time is long.
But even so he still stays young.
This little room where he must stay.
Will grow on him day by day.

All the time he wants time to end.
Until the cell becomes his friend.
When the lifer's not feeling well.
He'll crave the company of his cell.

The lifer loves this little room.
For it's his friend and it's his tomb.
There is no bus, he has no car.
He never ventures very far.